"In grief, there is joy; for we are closer to you."

Although known for speaking through movement in ways words sometimes can't communicate, she would often sit in stillness and let her pen dance on pages with her right hand as its dance partner.

Her voice carries legacy. Her words be testimony of who she was, affirmation of who she is, and a glimpse of who she's becoming.

She's beaming...

*She's growing, she's shedding, she's sharing
She is love.*

Understatement...

She is a universe who brings light to any dark space and amplifies an already bright room.

Hear her voice...

I'm sorry if
to you
I am not the same person I used to be.
And by sorry
I mean mostly to save a space for you
to mourn the loss of the image
of me
that you cling too tightly in your fist.
I pray you find the grace to let her go,
and give peace to myself in case you
can't accept
or refuse to see the me that exists today.
I also acknowledge that I am ever
changing
and shifting
and shedding
and returning,
and will be brand new again tomorrow to greet you if
you remain.

I open my mouth
Through my pen
And words blend meaning
To smooth milk
Make sense of what
My brain can't convey
Here
Intuition turns digits to messenger

I'm more Yellowjacket than bee
Find myself quick to draw a stinger instead of
responding with honey
Maybe it's the scorpion in me
Defense mechanisms ready
From a life of being called to meet
Unrealistic expectations
Standards you have to fly to reach
So needing help or not knowing
Feels like the ultimate breach

Maame

To miss a land I briefly knew in person
Stirs a grief
Ancestral in tone
Felt deep in arms
A movement of the pelvis
Concrete walls like the ones that housed me
A sadness unexpected
A motherland unconfirmed
The motherland
Felt like my mother's land
I've never seen
But a soul stirring
On soil
I still carry deep--
Bone deep
Soul deep--
A tug I can only describe as
Grief
A missing I can only compare
To the one who just left me
Mother's mother
My other motherland
One who created me
Stardust
In a universe
Layer to become my own galaxy
Layers of soil
Like the first between fingertips
Trailing across the garden
Created in her name
Mother
Land
Cradle me

And I will continue
To sit
On gold coin throne
While you walk around looking
For dollar bills
Paper money
I give you honey
But you call it bee spit
So I'll clean my wings
And stretch out
In the sun
Loneliness and silence
Must turn into a certain
Type of bliss
A fate better than this.

My heart aches
something vicious
tears at the surface

I wonder if you could bear
to see me
cry?

They tell me I'm strong
But strength shouldn't
tear me apart like this
If strength
hurts this much
I'd rather let
weakness
paralyze me.

Do you even let
your neurons
play my sweet memory?

Do your lips
hum
with expectation of words
spoken not so long ago?

If pain is healing
I'd rather be numb.

*She's human in this earthly world
Every storm shakes up the ancestral trees
the leaves that leave leave physical anxiety
Constantly branching
Rooting deeper
The coldest winter was prolly 45 degrees Fahrenheit a little past December
But felt like 35…
It gets cold in New Orleans…
But when it warms up
And those new leaves illuminate green
She glows along with them
Thanks to the suns warmth
Something she always carries with her…*

Vore

I devour large books in hours
Let the words run over me like a hot morning shower
Whole sentences caress my body like a sauna
As i get completely consumed with story lines
Characters divine twists and turns through their fictional worlds
I'm a little sadistic
Bending pages and hairline fractures to spines
Of books I'll re-read at least 5 times
I apologize
I'm a little bit of a masochist
Draining my eyes since I was 5
Forcing them to keep reading in the dimness of light
For hours
Exerting my power to transport to other worlds
Become other girls
Or men
Learn of new friends and lands that never end
People who use spirits like me to bend and mend and make sense of life
Divine
Books that make me contort my spine
Into weird shapes to get comfortable
Tucked and small enough to maybe try and fit into the front and back cover
Of my longest lover
The word.

Lineal

I am myself and not myself,
Am partway to who I am becoming
The mindful meditation of
Fruit divination,
And the careful bite of each selected cut
I am soaking in apple cider vinegar water
Gently purified before a wash
Impurities freckle the bowl.

They are a part of me,
Memories steeled away behind walls
Built to protect me
Shelter from love instead of

I am grief,
Skin sagging crevasse into frozen stare
It clings to my lungs
Makes puddle in cough
He claps my back to remind me
I am here
I am whole

I miss her still
Though I see her often
And i am so thankful
For her smile

'Ode' to MH at the Istanbul Cafe

I feel at peace in a place that's out of place
A space defined by my spirit, out of tune and time
I can feel it
I can almost touch and taste it
My soul…wants to bubble up
But my skin can't take the leap
Risk feels like free falling

You asked me to go skydiving
But how can I find home in the falling?
Can I find grace in the landing?
Serenity in the clouds?

Words don't come easily
To those so used to being silenced
They've sat so long inside that sentences have crumbled,
Words shattered
Until letters, half-syllables remain

Try to solve the puzzles in your own sweet time
Sometimes $1+1=1$
And sometimes 1 can be content in the living

She said "Time asks no questions."
It just is
No changing. You can't bargain with it
She just keeps on ticking away
Hours, minutes, years
Her infinity comes too soon

A breath ago I was a fetus
An exhale later, 22
When did I learn to fly?
A heartbeat ago I could barely crawl

A heartbeat ago I was single
Solitary
Used to an empty bed
Filling my time with my own imprints
Now
You've left fingerprints on my waist
Kisses on my thigh
Bites on my neck
And a warmth in my gut
You're becoming
Familiar

You've walked in
Arms wide open
And embraced me.
No matter how hard I fight
You refuse to let go
You loosen your hold
But you won't release me

Shall I fold into you?
Hands intertwined
Eyes locked
You study me
Shall I be an open book?

Will you lie to me?
Mesmerize me?
My heart is unfolding
Ocean pouring into you
Will you receive me?

You study me
With fingertips
Eyes
Lips
You constantly memorize
The lines you've exposed
Peeling away to my core

Will you heal me?
Or just steal from me,
A thief in the moonlight
Leaving an exposed shell
Where a house used to be

Will you kiss my soul?
Let me feel you in my breath
My eyelashes
Tickle my nose
Let your laughs dance across my spine
Your smiles kiss my temple

Your love leaves me dizzy,
Like palm wine
A high too pleasurable to describe
They say I'm hopeless
Heart too full of sunshine
Is my party too wild for your space?
Your rules can't contain me
My moonshine will knock you off your feet.

(I've turned into that hopeless artist
The one with the notebook at the bar
But I've never been so inspired!)

Matrilineal

I eat mangoes like my grandmother,
pressing thumb pads into flesh
delicately,
resisting a surgeon nick into the juices
palpating the seed
freeing it of the juice inside

I bite a small hole in the top
and squeeze carefully
Nectar flowing into my mouth
until all that remains
is skin clung to seed

I eat chicken like my mother,
paring meat from bone
gristle from joint;
Split in half and marrow sucked dry
Yes, I know there is more chicken,
but this one must be fully worshipped
and laid bare

I grow like my aunt,
beds fill of
married man's pork
and poor man's thyme.
Cucumbers
abundance
calls me home.

The tree shimmers
Leaves captured from termites
That seek sustenance
An offering for their meal
That leaves the trunk
Shimmering
Every time the wind takes a breath

The Fly

My room holds so many memories
I guess it's too full for Mom to go in
She never talks to me. Her eyes are stuck on the fly.
Little black speck, gracefully
buzzing around the room.
He dips and sways
a divine dance around my room.
He seems to read
the one blue speck under
the windowsill that we
missed from repainting the room,
the laughter from our paint fight.
He flies past me at
my stool in the corner by the window,
painting a picture of the
butterfly I told her about the day before.

He buzzes again, probably
talking to himself, and then
takes off
gray streaking his little feet
the big chalk outline still etched on the ground
Mom is jerked to breath, finally looking past the fly.
She sees the memory imprinted
on the floor. She looks up a bit, and finally
seems to see me, her little girl.
A memory that can't be washed away
as easily as blood and chalk.
But she blinks and I am gone.
And the room is too full again,
and she closes the door and
leaves me again with the memories in my room, cold and
empty.

Like paella,
but so much better.
You add your African influence,
kissing me with your sweet spicy.
Shrimp lips
smothering my arms with kisses of green bell pepper and tomato,
Leaving the savory scent of chicken on my stomach,
peppering my inner thighs,
until they quiver with Tony Cachere's
and spill over with rice.
Overflowing with the Cajun goodness
of a late-night cooking session.

I was your Adam&+you were my Eve
and this love we had was the fruit on the tree, this
knowledge we had
slipped from our grasp into
darkness
which in turn opened my heart's clasp.

In tumble the days
I played music that your limbs
took on as their own,
notes wrapping around arms
and hearts melting from my mouth to your sleeves.

Out poured the nights alone
holding tight to a memory
like it was a blanket
dragon's breath pulsing through veins
that drip with the sweet breath of magic.

and,

I slowly turn over this hourglass in my mind
each and every yellow grain
painting a memory into place.

*…Mix in some sensuality
A little dominance and submission
Switching from dancer to Domme
Or both at the same damn time
Ms. Mxen or Synamin Vixen
Here's to her humble beginnings…*

Tall
My chocolate epiphany
Height 6'2"
A sexy stance
Sweet caramel eyes
That burn with a passionate curiosity
Nose blends in
With lips as soft and round
As the sigh that escapes
When he kisses me
His hair a testament to royal ancestry
Roots tracing back
To the beat of the African drums
And the island steel pans
Strong
Masculine
Both close and not
His hands hold me
Conquering every curve and freckle
Of my skin
Becoming friends
With the dip of my back
The curves of my hips
Thighs and beyond

I looked into his eyes and drowned
Thought I died but woke up in the eye of the hurricane
Surrounded by calm oceans of purple waves

Clear

Epiphany

His voice touches me
Like a cold rush to the head,
Awakening my senses.

Curiosity ripens deep in my chest,
Spilling depth and breadth
Of my mind over his matter.

Bass overflows from his lips,
Mixing chocolate vibrations
With my caramel serenity

It grazes my hip,
Kisses the inner soul
Of my feet

My senses are sharpened
By his baritone blade
Soft as plush,
The cacophony of sweet nothings
Whispered in my ear

My body would be confused
If my heart wasn't so attuned
To the music that freely
Flows from his eyes

Voice and gaze blend
Into the sigh that escapes
From my lips

As i reach epiphany
Realizing the true essence
Of him

My Dominus has dope dick
My doe eyes dilate just thinking about it
When he says, clothes strip, legs split, and he
Commands and controls every bit of my clit

I love it
Can't help but gasp when he smacks my ass
I melt for him…

He reaches for me in his sleep
And when our bodies align
A remembrance travels up my spine
Each thrust hitting spots only a king with a
wide third eye could reach
Praising me while I grab at sheets
The type of freak who gets orgasms
Auracly
Tantra shit
He hit me with tantric dick
Man…

Orgasm feels like
The Big Bang snapped her fingers
And constellated.

The Experience

I miss the snap
Of flogger to flesh
The tickle i trickle
Across thighs and breast
I miss playing with rhythm
And suspense
Pausing before the loudest slap
Kisses the cup of your ass

I miss being asked
"May you?"
The sweetest gift
To give of flesh for me to partake
I miss the way I got to make
Them shudder

I miss the way we reclaimed space
Blackness adorning the room
Like the crown on my head
Body dripping happiness
And clothed with my name
So you call it with the respect
It deserves

I learned that I'm in love with my hands
The way they clap when I'm excited
Turn glutes to drums
I like the warmth of my hands
When I land just the right sting
To thighs screaming out for pain

I learned
That my hands could give variety

I made them sing with the music
And taught you polyrhythm
Suspense punctuating the space between
smacks

And we laughed
I revealed
That I don't need to be stern
To command the respect
I deserve
That to be me
Silly
Excited
Full of love and warmth
Allows for one to be trusting
In their submission
Allowed them to be felt
And welcomed

I miss being welcomed
To take control
In the dungeon

www.ingramcontent.com/pod-product-compliance
Lightning Source LLC
Chambersburg PA
CBHW072023290426
44109CB00018B/2324